THE DONNER MONUMENT

ASCENT TO THE PASS

The grade constructed in 1923 still (1960) loops laboriously upward
toward the Observation Point, Memorial Bridge, and highest point
(just off picture to the left). The difficulty of the passage for emigrant wagons is here strikingly demonstrated.

THE OLD SACRAMENTO TRAIL NORTH OF DONNER LAKE.

DONNER PASS

and those who crossed it

The story of the country
made notable by the *Stevens Party*, the *Donner Party*,
the *Gold-hunters*, and the *Railroad Builders.*

*With old and new illustrations
showing the Pass in summer and winter.*

By

GEORGE R. STEWART

Published by
THE CALIFORNIA HISTORICAL SOCIETY
San Francisco, California

IN THIS SERIES

Fabulous San Simeon, by Oscar Lewis. Illustrated with many beautiful photographs by Philip Negus Frasse. Paper, $1.50.

Los Angeles from the days of the Pueblo, by W. W. Robinson. Illustrated with many old and modern pictures, five in full color, plus map. Paper, $1.50; cloth, $4.00.

Donner Pass, by George R. Stewart. Illustrated. Paper, $1.95.

Exclusive Distributor

LANE PUBLISHING CO.

Publishers of Sunset Magazine and Books
Menlo Park, California

Society members should order directly from the Society. California purchasers must add four per cent sales tax.

ALSO BY GEORGE R. STEWART

Bret Harte	Fire
Ordeal By Hunger	U.S. 40
Storm	The Opening of the California Trail
Names on the Land	Pickett's Charge

COPYRIGHT 1960
CALIFORNIA HISTORICAL SOCIETY
2090 JACKSON STREET · SAN FRANCISCO, CALIFORNIA

LIBRARY OF CONGRESS
CATALOG CARD No. 60-8367

DESIGNED BY LAWTON KENNEDY

LITHOGRAPHED BY
HOOPER PRINTING & LITHOGRAPH COMPANY

AUTHOR'S NOTE

In the preparation of this book I have drawn heavily upon my own forty years of knowledge of the country. I wish to thank, for coöperation and courtesies received, the California State Library, Bancroft Library, California Division of Highways, California Historical Society, Southern Pacific Company, Organizing Committee of the VIII Olympic Winter Games, and U. S. Weather Bureau. I wish to thank, for various kinds of help, Andy Anderson, Carroll D. Hall, Robert Hancocks, Jr., George L. Harding, J. S. Holliday, Lester S. Konitz, Aubrey Neasham, Hal O'Flaherty, Allen R. Ottley, C. E. Peterson, Jack P. Stowe, and John B. Tompkins. The maps are the work of Jane Bendix.

Those further interested in the background may be referred to the following books. On the Stevens Party: *The Opening of the California Trail* (Moses Schallenberger's narrative); on the Donner Party: George R. Stewart, *Ordeal by Hunger;* on the gold mines: Joseph Henry Jackson, *Anybody's Gold;* Rodman W. Paul, *California Gold;* on the railroad: E. L. Sabin, *Building the Pacific Railway;* Oscar Lewis, *The Big Four;* on various aspects: *From Trails to Freeways* (Centennial Edition of *Calif. Highways and Public Works*); George R. Stewart, *U. S. 40;* N. E. A. Hinds, *Evolution of the California Landscape;* G. B. Sudworth, *Forest Trees of the Pacific Slope;* E. G. Gudde, *California Place Names;* George and Bliss Hinkle, *Sierra-Nevada Lakes.*

All motorists should visit Donner Memorial State Park, two miles west of Truckee, associated with the stories of Schallenberger and the Donner Party. (See half-title page for a picture of the Pioneer Monument, and other pictures in the text.) The great rock, marking the site of the Murphy cabin, can be visited. Funds have been appropriated for the erection of a museum, which will display relics of the Donner Party and will demonstrate as its main theme the influence of the Sierra barrier upon the development and continuing life of California.

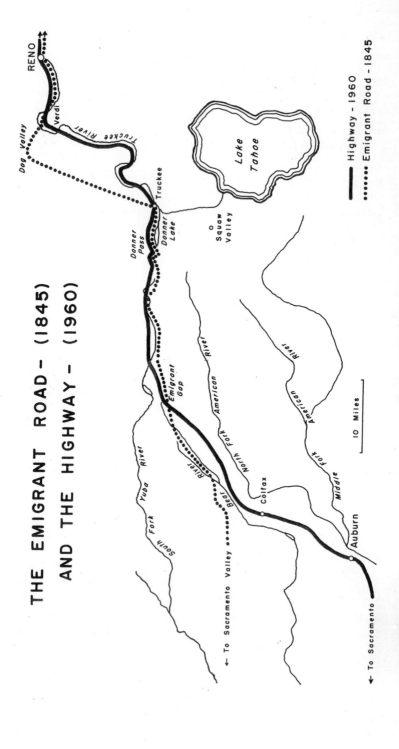

THE EMIGRANT ROAD — (1845)
AND THE HIGHWAY — (1960)

Highway - 1960
Emigrant Road - 1845

RENO

Dog Valley

Verdi

Truckee River

Lake Tahoe

Truckee

Donner Pass

Donner Lake

Squaw Valley

Emigrant Gap

American River

North Fork

American River

Middle Fork

Auburn

Colfax

Yuba River

South Fork

Bear River

To Sacramento Valley

To Sacramento

10 Miles

Donner Pass

and those who crossed it

Donner Pass, as it is now, you can see for yourself. This book attempts, by text and pictures, to give some idea of what you cannot see, of what lies in the past — of the men, women, and children of the Stevens Party, who first struggled through, of those of the Donner Party who starved and died by the lake, of the Forty-niners who came for gold, of hard-driving Charlie Crocker and his swarming Chinese who built the railroad, and of some things that have happened in the more recent years.

Before 1844, there were only Indians. On the east side, extending south of Lake Tahoe and east beyond Reno, lay the territory of a small tribe called the Washo. On the west side, with villages near both Colfax and Auburn, lived the Maidu. In early times both these tribes, as well as many others, were known to the white people by the derogatory term "diggers." In so far as this meant anything specific at all, it was probably that these Indians were often seen digging in the ground for roots or burrowing animals. They were not warlike and did not wear fine eagle-feather bonnets, and by modern standards they were a poverty-stricken lot, living squalidly. Still, they made beautifully artistic baskets.

Scarcely any Indians now live in the area, and about the only traces of them left are what are known as petroglyphs. These are crude little symbols or drawings — not unlike our "stick-drawings" — which they scratched or pecked into smooth rock-surfaces. Some petroglyphs still show on the granite below the top of the pass, but you cannot see them unless you know where to look, and are lucky enough to have good light.

After the Indians, in the West, the first discoverers were generally trappers, or explorers like Frémont. In later years, after Donner Pass had become famous, various trappers said that they had discovered it, but their claims cannot be accepted.

Thus, strangely, one of the most important of all the western passes was found by people who by all rights should have been traveling a well-known route, that is, by covered-wagon emigrants, comprising not only men but also women, and even children.

MOSES SCHALLENBERGER
(Aged about 60.)

ELISHA STEVENS
(Aged about 80.)

The Stevens Party set out from Council Bluffs, Iowa, in May, 1844. They traveled the well-established Oregon Trail as far as Raft River in southern Idaho, and there branched off on the dim traces of three wagons which the famous trapper Joe Walker had tried to take to California the year before. The party now consisted of twenty-six men, eight women, and probably seventeen children. They had eleven ox-drawn wagons, and the usual riding-horses, loose cattle, and dogs. Since there was hardly any road at all, they made slow progress. In September they began to follow down the Humboldt River, the route of U. S. 40, and about October 1 they arrived at Humboldt Sink, south of the present Lovelock, Nevada.

Here the wheel tracks that they were following kept on to the south, but Elisha Stevens, their astute leader, apparently wanted to head directly for California. So the emigrants consulted a local Indian chief whom they called Truckee. He told them that by going across the desert to the west they would come to a fine river. They did so, and out of gratitude called the river by the chief's name.

The emigrants then broke trail for their wagons up along the river, much as U. S. 40 now goes. Above Truckee Meadows (the open valley where Reno stands) they found the canyon very difficult. Sometimes they had to travel in the bed of the river, and they could average only about two miles a day. By now, they knew that they were struggling against time, to get across the mountains before winter.

About the middle of November they came to a place where the canyon which they had been following turned off toward the south, a direction they did not want to go. They camped where a small stream (Donner Creek) flowed into the Truckee River, and there they held a council. They decided to split up, and thus increase their chances. Two women and four men, all young and active, well-armed and well-mounted, were sent on up the canyon, to travel fast and try to get over the mountains before the snow got too deep. Three young men were assigned to stay with six of the wagons and build a cabin below where the creek flowed out of a fine mountain lake; there they would winter. The rest of the party—nineteen men, six women, and all the children—were to try to get over a pass with five wagons.

After several days of scouting, they decided to go along the north side of the lake and then to try the little gap just about where the railroad now goes through. Already there were two feet of snow on the pass.

They went ahead, by a route which no one has ever been able to work out very exactly. To take wagons up anywhere without a made road seems an impossibility. Their worst place was about half-way up, where there was "vertical rock about ten feet high." Here they even thought they would have to abandon the wagons. But they managed to find a little rift in the rock, and through it they forced the oxen one by one. Then they yoked the oxen again, put chains down over the cliff to the wagons, and with the oxen pulling from above, and the men heaving up from below, they brought the wagons one by one over the ledge. Eventually they reached the top of the pass.

The three young men then went back to build their cabin, and the others pushed on westward, still having to break trail over rough country. They went on across the valley where Lake Van Norden now is, and then kept to the high ground south of the line of the railroad. After two or three days' travel, they came down a rough steep hill, crossed the Yuba River twice, and encamped. Here, probably on November 28, a big snow storm struck them. About the same time, one of the

THE STEVENS PARTY CROSSING THE PASS

From a painting by Andrew P. Hill, 1878. The scene is realistically represented, but the wagons have been made to follow the line of the later road. The Indian supplies a romantic touch. Actually, there was snow on the pass at the time of this crossing.

women was taken in labor, and a baby girl was born. She was named Elizabeth Yuba Murphy, thus in her middle name commemorating that they were then camped by the Yuba River. Quite possibly they were near what is now Big Bend Ranger Station.

Since the snow prevented further progress, the men built a cabin, and left there all the women and children and two men. Then the other seventeen men went ahead through the snow, and eventually got to Sutter's Fort, where Sacramento now stands. Although this seems a kind of desertion, probably it was the best plan, because supplies were short; the women and children would have a better chance if the men were not there to take their share of the food.

In the meantime, the two women and four men who had gone up the canyon on horseback had come out on the shore of a beautiful mountain lake; they thus became the first white people ever to reach the shore of Lake Tahoe, though Frémont had already seen it from the mountains. But the six did not spend much time admiring the view. They pressed on down the west shore some miles, and then followed one of the streams up. They crossed the divide before the big snow storm struck, and then followed the water down. They had plenty of difficulty with the rough country, and were often short of food, but eventually managed to get through safely to Sutter's Fort.

There were also the three young men who stayed to watch the wagons left near Donner Lake. They built themselves a small log cabin at or near the site of the present Pioneer Monument, thinking that they could spend the winter pleasantly enough, supporting themselves by hunting. One of the three was eighteen-year-old Moses Schallenberger, from whom we have the story and whose name, with justice, now stands on Schallenberger Ridge, which looks down upon Donner Lake from the south. As he wrote later: "Knowing that we were not far from California, and being unacquainted, except in a general way, with the climate, I did not suppose that the snow would at any time be more than two feet deep, nor that it would be on the ground continually."

They soon found out better! When the storm came, snow fell until the cabin was almost covered. They immediately saw that they could get nothing from hunting, and so they killed the two half-starved cows that had been left with them. But the meat from the cows would not keep them through the winter, even if they could escape freezing to death. So they dried the meat, and also made crude snowshoes, utilizing some

VIEW EASTWARD FROM THE TOP OF THE PASS

Railroad snowsheds and pre-1923 "highway" at right; the 1960 high-way in center and at left. The emigrants probably took their wagons up the granite slope running from left to right and joining the pre-1923 road.

of the pliant hickory strips which supported the canvas of the covered wagons. They then started off over the pass through the snow. They got to the top by evening, but Schallenberger, who was only a gawky lad, was exhausted and ill. They spent a sleepless night, shivering with the cold, although their fire kept them from freezing.

In the morning Schallenberger realized that he could not go on, and that his only chance (and not a very good one) was to make it back to the cabin and try to live through the winter there alone. As he told the story, "We did not say much at parting. Our hearts were too full for that. There was simply a warm clasp of the hand accompanied by the familiar word, 'Good-by'." Then he started off by himself, with his comrades' last words ringing still in his ears, "Good-by, Mose!"

The two went ahead, and after some hardships managed to get to Sutter's Fort.

Schallenberger barely managed to drag himself back to the cabin, and was so tired that he had to take his foot in his hand to lift it across the door sill. The next morning, he felt a little better. Though despondent and having little hope of living through till spring, he still resolutely set about seeing what he could do for himself. Realizing that he could not exist very long on the small amount of beef that was left, he went out to try to shoot some game, but saw none, though there were plenty of fox-tracks. He then remembered that there were some traps in one of the wagons. He set the traps, using the heads of the cows for bait.

The next morning, he found that he had caught a coyote. It was thin and half-starved, but the boy tried roasting it and eating it. Even in his hunger he could not stomach the meat. During the next three days he tried cooking it in various ways, but still could not make it edible. Then he caught two foxes in his traps. When he roasted the meat of one of them, he was amazed and delighted to find it delicious.

He continued trapping as the weeks passed—sometimes catching coyotes, and sometimes foxes. The coyotes he hung

THE TRUE PASS

The lowest passageway is through this gap, which is here seen, looking west. From bottom to top, at right, the pre-1923 road, the Dutch Flat-Donner Lake road, the 1960 highway. Weather station at right; high: way maintenance buildings in center. The emigrants took their wagons along the winding road at the left, crossing at an altitude of about 7050 feet.

up, as a reserve of food, if worst came to worst. Eventually he had eleven carcasses thus hanging, frozen stiff. Once he shot a crow, but found it as bad eating as a coyote. The foxes he continued to cook and eat, often having little but never running out.

He was alone. Most of the time he was penned within the cabin, since the snow remained too deep for getting about. As he wrote later, "My life was more miserable than I can describe. The daily struggle for life and the uncertainty under which I labored were very wearing." Fortunately there were some books in one of the wagons, and he was able to spend much time poring over them. He would read aloud to break the terrifying stillness, and sometimes he merely talked to himself.

One evening a little before sunset about the last of February, he was standing a short distance from the cabin, and made out the form of a man coming toward him through the trees. At first he thought it was an Indian, but soon he recognized Dennis Martin, one of his companions in the wagon-train. At the urging of Schallenberger's sister, Martin had come across the pass on snow shoes to see what had happened to the boy.

Martin, who was a Canadian and accustomed to snow shoes, soon manufactured some better ones than the makeshift contraptions that Schallenberger had first used. Thus equipped, the two of them crossed the pass, and soon joined the party containing the women and children. Some of the men had now rejoined this group, and they all then made their way to the Sacramento Valley.

The Stevens Party thus suffered no deaths, and entered California two stronger than when setting out, because of a baby born in the Rocky Mountains, and another at the camp on the Yuba. Their success may be partially attributable to good luck, but is also in large extent owed to the courage and sagacity of the emigrants and to their exceptional leader. The pass over which he took the wagons should in all justice have been called Stevens Pass.

Later in the spring, some of the men returned and brought the wagons out. Those left at the lake-cabin had been plundered after the departure of Schallenberger, but the Indians had not taken the firearms, realizing that these were dangerous to handle.

The opening of the California Trail may thus be assigned to the years 1844 and 1845. In the former year, wagons were taken over the pass; in the latter year, all the way to the Sacramento Valley. Although many relocations have since been

TRACE OF WAGONS

Buttress roots of old trees along the trail failed to renew themselves
after having the bark ground off by passing wheels.

BEAR VALLEY FROM THE EAST

The valley offered a comfortable campsite with good grazing, and so lured the emigrants down from the ridge. California Highway No. 20 ascends from the other side of the valley. The emigrants went to the lower end of the valley, and then worked up to a ridge, much as No. 20 now does.

made—and are still occurring—the general location of the present highway is a tribute to the indomitable will with which the Stevens Party pressed westward. From Humboldt Sink to Emigrant Gap the modern road follows their general route (see map), and is seldom more than a mile or two away.

In 1845 the Ide Party set out for California. They made the first important relocation by turning off the trail of the Stevens Party at the site of Verdi, Nevada, and thus avoiding the difficult upper Truckee Canyon by passing through Dog Valley and returning to the first route near Truckee. At the pass their guide—the trapper Caleb Greenwood, who had been with the Stevens Party—advised them to take their wagons apart and carry them up piecemeal. Not liking this idea, the men scouted around, found a barely passable route, and put some work on it by rolling stones away and cutting trees. They then had a trail wide enough for one wagon, going up the pass in a series of steep ascents with slightly flatter places between. They took the wagons across by the process of driving the oxen up to the flatter places, letting chains down to the wagons below, and thus hitching the wagons up step by step.

News that the route to California was practicable inspired a great immigration in 1846. When large parties with dozens of wagons began to arrive at the foot of the pass, the result must have been a traffic jam—the first of the many that have plagued travelers since then. Doubtless for this reason an alternate route was worked out—by way of Coldstream Canyon, and thus over the crest at a point a mile and a half farther south. This is now sometimes called merely "the emigrant route," though it is actually not the original one.

The large migration of 1846 is chiefly remembered for the misadventures of the Donner Party. This group of emigrants, from Illinois and other mid-western states, had originally been a part of the great migration, but after crossing the crest of the Rocky Mountains they organized as a separate party under the captaincy of George Donner, a sixty-two-year-old farmer from

THE GAP FROM BEAR VALLEY

From the level meadow one looks up at the steep 600-foot slope down which the emigrants lowered their wagons by ropes snubbed around trees. Though the landmarks have been lost because of much excavation for both railroad and highway, the "gap" was probably at the place here marked by a patch of white snow lying on the railroad fill which has blocked the old passageway.

CHARLES T. STANTON
(Aged about 30.)

JAMES F. REED
(Aged about 50.)

Springfield, Illinois. At the same time they decided to travel by
way of the so-called Hastings Route. When all its members had joined, the party consisted of eighty-seven persons—
twenty-seven men, seventeen women, and forty-three children.
They were distributed among twenty-three wagons.

Their troubles began soon. They were persuaded to cut a
new road across the Wasatch Mountains, and lost much time.
They lost more time in crossing the Salt Lake Desert and in
following a circuitous route farther west. Donner proved a not
very effective captain, and much of the leadership devolved
upon James F. Reed, who was energetic, but also hot-tempered.
Having knifed a man, Reed was banished from the company,
though he could plead self-defense. Other personal difficulties
occurred, but it is not likely that these quarrels delayed the
progress. Toward the end of October the party approached
the pass, traveling in three sections, the last section consisting
of the Donners themselves, perhaps two days' journey behind
the leading wagons.

On the night of October 31, the emigrants in the advance
section camped not far from Schallenberger's cabin. An inch
of snow lay on the ground. On the pass ahead, they could see
that the snow was deep. A storm was threatening.

Next day they went ahead, but found the snow five feet deep on the approaches of the pass. Being unable to keep on the trail, they could do nothing but turn the wagons about, and bring them back. They camped that night at the cabin. Rain fell heavily the next day, and they remained in camp, hoping that the rain would wash the snow away, though actually the rain would be snow at higher levels. That evening the second section arrived.

RIDGE BEYOND BEAR VALLEY

From Bear Valley the emigrants mistakenly brought their wagons to the top of this narrow and broken-topped ridge to the north. Much of the way the road followed right along the narrow crest.

Next day a few of the people were discouraged and remained where they were. The others started with their wagons, but soon realized these would have to be abandoned. They then packed some goods on their oxen, and started ahead on foot, floundering in deep snow as they drove the oxen, or else on horseback or muleback, almost everyone carrying a child. They got nearly to the top of the pass, but darkness was coming on and the women were exhausted. They camped in the snow, and that night a foot of snow fell on top of them.

In the morning, beaten, they made their way back and reassembled at the cabin.

The Donners in the rear section had not even managed to get so far. They were overtaken by the snow, and made makeshift camps on Alder Creek about five miles back on the trail.

On this day, November 4, the emigrants were thoroughly discouraged, but were not panic-stricken, or in immediate fear for their lives. They had some confidence that they could build log cabins, slaughter their remaining cattle, and thus live until spring. They expected that the snow would melt between storms, as it did in the Middle West, and that they could then hunt game.

CROSS-COUNTRY VIEW

Here seen from the air, the rugged nature of the country appears. On the narrow ridge the white line shows a still used road on the trace of the emigrant trail. The canyon of Bear River lies beyond, and then the town of Dutch Flat with its "diggings." Still farther off is the railroad, with the modern highway just beyond it.

The Breen family, apparently having got there first, occupied the cabin, which thus came to be known as the Breen cabin. The two others, from the names of the most numerous families living in them, were known as the Murphy and Graves cabins.

While the emigrants labored, rain and slushy snow continued to fall, day after day. Their hastily-built, squat log cabins, roofed with tents and wagon-canvases and ox-hides, could be kept warm enough, but food was short, and the snow on the pass was getting deeper and deeper.

The storm did not cease until November 11, and by that time the men and women knew that their situation was desperate. Even counting some mules and some trail-worn cattle not yet slaughtered, there was not enough food to get everybody through until spring. One of their hunters was lucky enough to kill a bear. The only other game to be bagged consisted of a coyote, an owl, and two ducks. The plight of the Donners was equally bad. They had pitched their tents and built rough huts, so that their situation for shelter was rather worse than that of those at the lake, and for food they were no better off.

The only solution was for some of the strongest to attempt to escape across the pass, thus leaving more food for those who remained. So, on November 12, the very first clear day, fifteen of the adults made a try. They found the snow too deep, and had to return before they had even been gone for one night.

During nine days of clear weather the snow consolidated somewhat and on November 21, twenty-two people set out, including six women and three half-grown children. They crossed the pass, and spent one night camped just beyond it. Then they became discouraged, and turned back.

More storms followed, until Patrick Breen, keeping a diary, recorded on December 13 that the snow was eight feet deep on the level. At this time occurred another disaster, for which the people themselves were partly to blame. The remaining cattle and mules, not being carefully penned up or watched, wandered off, were covered with snow, and died in places where their bodies could not be found. The best reserve of food was thus lost.

During the period of storms, many of the emigrants had worked at manufacturing snowshoes from the ox-bows. On December 16, when the weather at last had cleared, seventeen people started for the pass. Two of them gave up and returned that same day. Ten men and five women kept on, thus becoming the group sometimes known as "the Forlorn Hope." They carried six days' scanty rations. They could make but slow progress, taking two days to get across the top of the pass. But they struggled on, since to return to the cabins offered no hope.

On the sixth morning, the chivalrous Charles F. Stanton, who had been lagging, felt that he was finished. Not to be a drag on his companions, he remained sitting by the fire, smoking his pipe, when the others went on.

The fourteen soon lost their way, wandering too far to the

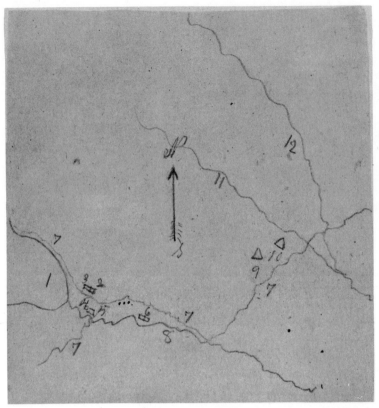

MAP BY A SURVIVOR

In 1879 W. C. Graves, who had passed through the experiences of the Donner Party as a lad of 18, drew this map from memory. Although there are mistakes of scale, the map is of value for its locations of roads, cabins, etc. He explained his numerals: 1) Lake, 2) Old cabin, 3) Keseberg's addition, 4) Rock, 5) Murphy's cabin, 6) Graves' cabin, 7) Roads, 8) Outlet [i.e., Donner Creek], 9, 10) Donner tents, 11, 12) Creeks. ' ' ' little springs coming out of hill and running down toward creek.

south and becoming entangled in the rough country of the American River canyons. They were now out of food. On the ninth day a storm broke, and they were forced to huddle beneath the shelter of a few blankets, for two days and two nights. Four of them died, and to gain strength to move forward, the others resorted to cannibalism.

They then struggled on—ragged, emaciated, exhausted and starving. They came to lower altitudes, where snow lay only in patches. There a luckily killed deer gave temporary relief. Three more of them died and their bodies were eaten.

The survivors at last struggled into a village of friendly Indians, and by them were passed along to the first ranch in the Sacramento Valley.

In this horrible yet heroic journey eight men died and only two survived. All five women came through. They had been thirty-three days on the trail.

California had at that time only a scattered population, and was in a disturbed state because of the Mexican War. Nevertheless, alerted by the arrival of the snowshoers, the people organized for the relief of the emigrants.

In the mountain camps, however, the situation had already become critical. Several deaths had occurred. A few families still had dried beef, but many were living on hides. These, if boiled long enough, yielded a kind of glue, which was slightly nutritious even if nauseous. Mrs. Reed, whose husband had been banished, killed the children's pet dog, little Cash. She and her four children lived on him for a week, eating everything but the bones. Mrs. Reed then made a desperate attempt, along with her twelve-year-old daughter and two adults, to escape across the pass. After spending four nights in the snow, they were forced to return. If they had not returned, they would have died in a five-day storm, which raised the level of the snow at the cabins to an estimated thirteen feet.

On the last day of January, a fifteen-year-old boy died. Several other people were failing rapidly. On this same day, however, a relief party started from the Sacramento Valley. This party at once encountered bad weather. By the time of leaving Bear Valley and entering the deep snow, it had been reduced to seven stalwart and heroic men. Carrying heavy packs of food, laboring along through deep snow, huddling around a fire during the bitterly cold nights, these seven floundered on, in daily danger of being trapped by a storm. They gradually lightened their packs by leaving caches to be picked up on the way back. Just before sunset on February 18, they arrived at the cabins, and were greeted like messengers from heaven by the starving people.

The rescue party distributed food sparingly, and prepared for a return journey. Three of them went on to the Donner tents, and brought back two adults and four of the older children. The party set out to return on February 22, expecting to live on the caches. The seven rescuers were shepherding three men, four women, and fifteen children, ranging down to three years old.

They found that the caches had been destroyed by preda-

THE BREEN DIARY (February 25-26, 1847)

From November 20, 1846 to March 1, 1847, Patrick Breen kept his famous diary of his experiences at the lake camp. The next to last page is here reproduced.

tory animals. Thus reduced to starvation, they struggled ahead. A man and a three-year-old girl died along the trail. The children, who could walk on the crust of the snow, often got along better than the adults. Pressing on, they at last met another relief party advancing, and were supplied with food.

THE BIG ROCK
The Murphy cabin was built by utilizing this rock for one side and thus forming a kind of natural fireplace. The plaque gives the names of the members of the Donner Party.

This second relief party was headed by Reed himself. His wife and two older children were with the refugees whom he thus fortunately rescued.

Since Reed still had two children at the lake, and was carrying food to all the emigrants, he went ahead vigorously. His party arrived at the lake on March 1, and immediately set about organizing for a return. Reed visited the Donner camp, and brought back three children. In both camps evidences of cannibalism were now apparent.

Reed began his return journey on March 3, with one man, two women, and fourteen children, ranging in age from fourteen to infancy. He had great difficulty in forcing the emaciated people to make much progress, but he hoped to reach his caches or else to meet another relief party. Only on the third day were they able to get across the pass, and go a little beyond

THE CAMP AT DONNER LAKE (NOVEMBER, 1846)
Drawn from a description furnished by a survivor, this picture is of some value in showing what the cabins were like. The conical object is the artist's conception of the big rock. Note the Graves' cabin (left) roofed with ox-hides. The old Schallenberger (Breen) cabin (right) is the only one not flat-roofed.

it. They camped that night on the edge of Summit Valley (now largely occupied by Lake Van Norden). That night a storm of extreme intensity broke.

The people huddled about a fire built on top of a platform of green logs on the deep snow. As the storm continued throughout the next day, the heat of the fire melted the snow, and the whole fire sank gradually, until it was burning at the bottom of a pit. In the high wind the cold was intense, and the men of the relief party labored to the point of exhaustion to supply firewood. Once the foundation logs shifted and precipitated most of the fire into the puddle of water beneath. Only by heroic exertions was the fire kept burning, and life thus maintained in the refugees. The storm continued. After the third night, one of the children was found to be dead. On March 8, the storm ceased, and the men of the relief party along with three children pressed on. The rest of the emigrants were too exhausted and discouraged to move ahead. They were left with some fuel, but no food was available.

Reed's party floundered on through the snow, suffering greatly, and eventually made contact with other men advanc-

ARRIVAL OF THE RELIEF PARTY

A companion piece to the preceding picture, this drawing shows the first relief party of seven men arriving at the cabins on February 18, 1847. The snow was at this time about 13 feet deep, and the people are properly shown as emerging from the cabin through a hole in the snow.

ing. This third relief party found eleven refugees still living around the fire in the pit of snow. Three had died, and again the survivors had had to resort to cannibalism.

Some of the men in the relief party brought these eleven back to safety. The others pushed on across the pass. By this time, only a few remained alive at the cabins—almost their only food, the bodies of those who had already died. Conditions at the Donner tents were equally bad. George Donner was dying, and his wife Tamsen heroically refused to leave him. The relief party returned, bringing out the three young daughters of George and Tamsen Donner, and one young man. Those who remained were the dying George Donner, his wife Tamsen, old Mrs. Graves, and a German named Keseberg.

A party which went across in the spring to salvage the goods in the wagons found all of these dead except Keseberg. According to the reports of these men, he was well fed and well nourished.

Of the eighty-seven emigrants, five had died before reaching the mountain camps, thirty-four either there or upon the mountains, and one just after reaching the valley. Many of the

TALL STUMPS

Tall stumps were for many years a notable landmark around the Donner camps. These in the picture are at least 12 feet tall, so that the snow must have been about that deep when they were cut. The location of this picture is unknown. It may be near the lake cabins, or it may be near "Starved Camp" in Summit Valley.

PATTY AT THE ROCK

At the dedication of the monument in 1918 "Little Patty" (Martha Reed) was almost eighty years old. Here, in somber widow's weeds, she looks at the great rock with which she was only too familiar during the winter of 1846-7.

forty-seven survivors bore physical or mental scars. The story is, at once, not only horrible, but also tragic and heroic in many of its aspects. Its spectacular qualities have resulted in the name Donner being fixed upon the whole region.

The disaster was primarily the result of the emigrants' bad judgment in taking the Hastings route, and thus losing much time. It was their bad luck, too, to encounter an unusually severe winter, with heavy snows on the pass as early as October 28. Some modern critics have maintained that their disaster resulted from their attempting Donner Pass instead of the Coldstream Canyon route, but the original documents give no such indication. If the alternate route offered easier grades, it crossed at a higher altitude and was also longer, and there is no reason to think that by attempting it they would have done any better. Once blocked by the snow, most of the emigrants displayed as much energy and initiative as could be expected, as is shown by the numerous attempts to escape across the pass on foot. But their failure to watch their cattle was unfortunate.

MODERN PYGMIES

At the dedication of the statue some of the on-lookers climbed up and stood beside the figures, thus doubtless demonstrating the heroic stature of the pioneers.

DEDICATION OF THE MONUMENT

On June 6, 1918, the Pioneer Monument at the lake camp was dedicated with proper ceremonies. Here photographed between the flags (left to right) are Gov. Emmet D. Boyle (Nevada), Mrs. Martha (Patty) Reed Lewis, Mrs. Eliza Donner Houghton, Mrs. Frances Donner Wilder, and Gov. W. D. Stephens (California). The three women were all survivors of the Donner Party. The inscription on the tablet reads: "Virile to risk and find; kindly withal and a ready help. Facing the brunt of fate; indomitable,—unafraid."

MRS. GRAVES' HOARD

When about to leave the lake camp in March, 1847, Mrs. Graves had the men of the rescue party remove several hundred dollars from its hiding-place in her wagon. At the first camping-place, part way along the north shore of the lake, she became doubtful of the honesty of her escort, and concealed the money in the woods. She died in Summit Valley a few days later. The money was discovered by chance in 1891, and here photographed.

PATTY'S DOLL

When eight-year-old Martha (Patty) Reed left the lake camp with the relief party on March 3, 1847, she carried with her a tiny doll, concealing it so that the grown-ups would not throw it away to lighten her load. When out of the snow, she brought it out again. She preserved the doll, and it eventually found its place in a museum.

TALL STUMPS AT ALDER CREEK
The last of the tall stumps to remain standing (1959) are those near the camp of the Donners on Alder Creek. These are about 9 feet tall.

Although some emigrants continued to use what was then called the Truckee route, the opening of other roads—particularly that through Carson Pass in 1848—reduced this original one to secondary status. The focus of interest during the Gold Rush thus must shift from the pass to the foothill country on the west slope.

After the original discovery at Coloma in January, 1848, prospectors fanned out in all directions. Gold was discovered near Auburn on May 16, 1848. These first discoveries were along the beds of streams, where the natural action of the water had been concentrating gold for many millenia. These deposits were often extremely rich, and could therefore be profitably worked merely with a pan. The introduction of this primitive instrument, which soon became symbolic of the whole Gold Rush, was traditionally credited to Mexican miners.

As the rush brought in its thousands from all over the world, the richer diggings were rapidly exhausted, and the history of gold-mining in California becomes the story of the introduction of methods by which larger and larger quantities of less

MINING IN AUBURN RAVINE—1852

This remarkably old picture is also remarkably good, considering the conditions under which it must have been taken. Since the exposure required many seconds, the people are "frozen" into position around their "long tom," and the scene becomes somewhat artificial. Note the rarity, "a live woman in the mines," and apparently a respectable one. The two men on the right seem to be identical twins.

HEAD OF AUBURN RAVINE—1852

Four Chinese with pigtails and big hats here share the picture with three other miners. This shows water running through a sluice-box and over its riffles. Stones have been placed to break the flow of the water. Note the substantial buildings of sawed lumber in the background, though the town was less than four years old.

MINER AT AUBURN—1852

Here the "long tom" is supplied with water by means of a hose.

and less rich material could be profitably handled. Miners from the gold fields of northern Georgia are credited with the introduction of the rocker and with the use of mercury. But the rocker itself was soon succeeded by the sluice-box, through which a continuous stream of water served to wash away the earth and leave the gold deposited behind the cleats nailed to its bottom. Gold which was imprisoned in quartz veins was first released by the primitive Mexican *arrastra*, merely a large stone dragged around in a circle by a mule. An improved form of arrastra consisted of a stone shaped into the form of a wheel and mounted on a pivot. Cornish miners, however, soon introduced the stamp mill, run by water or steam power, to crush the quartz more efficiently.

Along the road that descends from the pass, Auburn, Illinoistown (near Colfax), and Dutch Flat developed as typical mining camps.

As the stream workings began to peter out, prospectors turned their attention to the thick layers of red gravel on the tops of the ridges. These gravels were the deposits of ancient rivers, laid down in a past geological age. The concentration was so low that a man trying to wash gold with a pan would have starved to death. To move immense tonnages of gravel and thus collect appreciable quantities of gold, the method of hydraulic mining was developed.

METHODS OF MINING

Though late, romanticized, and synthesized, this drawing gives a good idea of some primitive methods of gold mining — pan, cradle or rocker, and arrastra using stones and mule-power.

HYDRAULIC DESTRUCTION

The picture, probably taken about 1890, gives some indication of what hydraulic mining did to the country. The scene is near Dutch Flat. Mining has apparently ceased, but the trestle bearing the huge pipe is still standing. Note the stumps of good-sized trees left lying about.

Nothing could be basically simpler. A large hose projecting water under high pressure was directed at a bank of gravel. As the bank was torn down, the water carrying the debris was run through sluice-boxes and the gold was collected. This was big business, and no game at which the lone miner could play. Flumes had to be constructed to bring water many miles from the headwaters of the rivers. Giant pipelines were necessary, to carry the water at high pressure; gigantic nozzles, from which it could be projected.

The attack upon these gravels was so vigorous that the face of the country was changed. The tops of the ridges were washed away, and gigantic scars of treeless gravel remained. After the gold had been extracted, all the "tailings" were washed down into the streambeds. The canyon of Bear River above the hydraulic workings of Dutch Flat is steep-sided and narrow; below, it is filled up with a broad and level expanse of gravel, at least 150 feet deep. This clogging up of the streams subjected the farm lands of the Sacramento Valley to silting and dangerous floods, and led to a conflict between mining and agricultural interests. By the 1880's, mining was a declining industry, and agriculture was advancing. In 1884 an epoch-making decision by Judge Lorenzo Sawyer required that tailings must be impounded—and this was seldom economical. A few small operations lingered on.

Spectacular evidences of hydraulic mining are still to be seen along the highway just north of Gold Run. The high red cliffs along one side were cut out by the hydraulic hoses, and mark the limits of their work. Here mining was halted because the railroad ran along the top of this piece of land. In fact, it still crosses a narrow isthmus between these Gold Run diggings on the south and the Dutch Flat diggings on the north.

On the side of the highway opposite the cliff, the diggings stretch away toward the canyon of the North Fork of the

SECRETTOWN TRESTLE

The now defunct Secrettown was a few miles west of Gold Run. The railroad first crossed the ravine by means of a hastily-built wooden trestle. Such structures were subject to fire (note barrels), and so were gradually replaced by fills. This remarkable picture (probably by Alfred Hart) was taken in 1877 during the process of filling. The one-horse dump-carts were still the standard means of moving dirt. Note the Chinese laborers in their big hats.

DUTCH FLAT HOTEL

Partly constructed in 1852, this hotel is one of the best remaining buildings of the Gold Rush period.

American River, which received the debris. After three quarters of a century the trees are finally managing to reëstablish themselves, but bare spaces of gravel can still be seen.

During the Gold Rush the Indians were largely killed off. In the winter of 1849-50 a gay company of young men of Illinoistown, calling themselves "the Blades," escaped boredom by forcing the Indians out of their nearby villages and driving them across Bear River, killing a good many of them in the process.

The life of the Gold Rush period was notoriously violent. The picturesquely nick-named Rattlesnake Dick—one of the famous California bandits—sometimes operated in the vicinity of Illinoistown. In a confused encounter on the road between Auburn and Illinoistown, during the night of July 11, 1859, he was shot down. The next morning a stage-driver found the bullet-riddled body by the roadside and brought it into Auburn, where it lay on the sidewalk as a curious crowd gathered around.

THE OLD PROSPECTOR

Why must a prospector always, in the West, be labeled as old? This one lacks gray hair, but his clothing at least is seedy enough to be called old. The contraption on the burro's back is probably some sort of machine for washing gold, fitted with wheels for easier moving. The picture is probably not early, since such outfits could still be seen as late as the 1920's. Many "snipers" worked their claims around Dutch Flat during the Depression years of the 1930's.

Throughout the 1850's the region of Donner Pass was almost unfrequented. The old emigrant road, never more than a make-shift affair, was rarely traveled, and probably became next to impassable because of washouts, landslides, and falling trees. This happened in spite of the fact that the men of the period were greatly interested in trans-Sierra roads. Many proposals sprang from local enterprise, since each of the larger towns tried to develop a road which would bring trade to it. The original route, however, was not viewed with favor. Even the Placer County Emigrant Road, promoted by Auburn, went farther to the south, following the ridge between the North and Middle forks of the American, and crossing the divide at the head of Squaw Valley. Elisha Stevens' old route would doubtless have lapsed into obscurity, if it had not been for two reasons—first, its natural advantages and second, the astuteness of Theodore D. Judah.

The natural advantages were two. Donner Pass leads directly, by way of the Truckee River and the Forty-mile Desert, to the Humboldt River, and this, in its turn, supplies the natural highway across most of Nevada, and therefore to the eastern United States. Besides being direct, this route offers a minimum of ups and downs. Consider the problem of getting across the canyon-seamed country of the Sierra Nevada. Unless you are willing continually to ascend and descend, you must either follow a canyon or one of the main ridges between river-systems. But because of the amount of side-hill excavation required, a canyon route was not practical for early roads.

THEODORE D. JUDAH   CHARLES CROCKER

So the roads generally followed ridges, although they were not always successful in avoiding ups and downs; thus the Placer County Immigrant Road had to descend from Auburn clear to the North Fork of the American and then climb out again—a procedure possible for a stage road, but quite out of the question for a railroad. Even worse was the situation on Johnson's Cut-off, the road which has now become U. S. 50. In the later fifties, it was the great trans-Sierra road, and the busy traffic between California and the Comstock mines passed over it. But this road, in addition to some ups and downs on the west side, passed one summit, dropped to the level of Lake Tahoe, and then had to climb again and again descend. But the broad-topped ridge passing through Auburn and then extending on toward Donner Pass lies between river systems, with the Bear and Yuba to the north and the American to the south. This means that there is no need of descending to cross any important stream.

These advantages impressed Theodore D. Judah, a Connecticut engineer who had come to California to help construct

CONSTRUCTION SCENE

This picture, probably of 1865 or 1866, shows construction work through a magnificent forest of pine and fir. Note one-horse dump carts and "shelf" grading, also to be seen in the following pictures.

the first railroad in the Sacramento Valley. In 1859 Dr. D. W. Strong of Dutch Flat urged Judah to investigate Donner Pass. The two of them rode across on horseback, and Judah recognized the advantages of the route for a railroad. He investigated elsewhere, crossing the mountains twenty-three times on foot, on horseback, or with a light one-horse wagon equipped with a compass, an odometer for measuring distances, and a barometer for estimating altitudes. His final decision was for Donner Pass.

He interested some Sacramento business men, and on June 27, 1861, the Central Pacific Company of California was incorporated. The famous "Big Four" of later days were connected with it—Leland Stanford, president; Collis P. Huntington, vice-president; Mark Hopkins, treasurer; Charles Crocker, a director. Judah was chief engineer.

Judah died in 1863, when the construction had scarcely been started. The Big Four carried on, but the only one of them who was associated with the actual building was Charles Crocker, the great Bull of the Woods.

Ground was broken at Sacramento on January 8, 1863. Because of the financial uncertainties, progress was slow at

FORT POINT CUT

The "shelf" grading method, used in heavy cuts to allow the employment of many carts at the same time, is here seen in use near Blue Canyon.

first, and the railroad took two years and four months to reach Auburn, only thirty-six miles.

At the same time, however, there was a new activity, and one which was to be of great importance in eventually establishing the Donner Pass route as that of a great highway. What

OWL GAP CUT

The "shelf" method is here seen with the carts actually in position. No power-tools were used in the construction of the railroad; all loading of carts was by hand-shoveling. Location: near Blue Canyon.

was known as "the head of wagon navigation," was then at Dutch Flat. The builders of the railroad reasoned that, as their railhead advanced, their route would become more and more economical for wagon traffic. They therefore decided to build a road across the mountains from Dutch Flat, to take over the freighting business to the Comstock mines. The result was the Dutch Flat-Donner Lake road, which stands in an interesting half-way position between the emigrant road and the modern highway.

From Dutch Flat it followed the ridge up, close to the line of U. S. 40, until at Emigrant Gap it connected with the emigrant trail. It followed this rather closely, on past Crystal Lake and beyond Big Bend. There it kept to the bottom land along the river, and did not take to the high country as the trail had done. The two rejoined however, in the vicinity of the pass, and from there on kept close together.

This road was opened in June, 1864. At once a busy traffic developed through Donner Pass. On July 16, the California

CLIFFS NEAR GOLD RUN

Close along the north side of the highway rise the cliffs of red gravel left when the hydraulic hoses stopped washing the country away for gold. Their height may be gauged by comparing them with the car.

Stage Company began to operate over it from what was then the railhead at Clipper Gap to Virginia City, in Nevada. As the railhead advanced, the pull for stages and wagons became shorter and shorter, and the route thus became more and more advantageous.

The railhead continued to advance slowly. On September 10, 1865, it reached the vicinity of the old mining camp, Illinoistown. The new station, however, was given the name Colfax from the highly popular Speaker of the House of Representatives, who inspected the new railroad that summer during a tour of the West.

Above Colfax, the builders encountered a very difficult problem in getting around the great promontory, high above the American River, that they named Cape Horn. At last, on Independence Day, 1866, the Central Pacific was officially opened to Dutch Flat, and thus made contact with the new road.

CHINESE TEA-CARRIER

A tea-carrier was employed to bring to his fellow-Orientals their favorite beverage during the construction of the railroad. He is here seen near the opening of a partially constructed tunnel.

Three and a half years had elapsed since the ground-breaking, and only sixty-seven miles of railroad were open. Moreover, the most difficult part of the construction—the granite-country of the pass, and the sheer descent toward Donner Lake—still remained ahead.

By now, financial problems had been solved, and the Central Pacific found itself in competition for land grants with the Union Pacific, which was building westward from Council

CRYSTAL LAKE HOUSE

Though by-passed by the railroad and the modern highway, beautiful Crystal Lake was on the emigrant trail and the Dutch Flat-Donner Lake road. This photograph was probably taken in 1866 when the railhead was at Dutch Flat and the great six- and eight-horse freight wagons were still moving over the road. All trace of this hotel has now vanished.

Bluffs. By now, also, "Charlie" Crocker had hammered his organization into shape, and was ready to put the pressure on. Since he found great trouble in getting laborers and keeping them on the job, he imported Chinese coolies by the thousand. They came to be known as "Charlie Crocker's pets," and most of the later work on the railroad was performed by them.

Crocker himself at this time was a magnificent physical specimen, almost six feet tall, weighing 260 pounds, boiling over with energy. He described himself in often-quoted words, "I used to go upon that road and went backwards and forwards ... like a wild bull, and everybody was afraid of me." He had no respect for the rights of labor, and once wrote, "no need of sympathy for those men. ... The only way to do was to rule them with an iron hand."

[47]

CISCO—1867

In this summer the railhead was at Cisco, and passengers for Virginia City were transferred at that point to six-horse Concord stages.

SNOW SHEDS UNDER CONSTRUCTION

In this picture the photographer, probably Alfred Hart, seems to have been chiefly interested in an artistic study of light and shadow. The location is near Emigrant Gap, in 1867.

THE SNOW PLOW—"AT WORK"

This somewhat fanciful drawing by G. M. Ottinger purports to represent a scene near Blue Canyon.

[49]

PACK TRAIN WITH FIREWOOD

For many years the locomotives burned wood, and whole mountain-sides were swept bare of trees for firewood.

OBSERVATION CAR AT CAPE HORN

For the photographer to get this picture (about 1870) the train was stopped and everyone looked out the windows and held still. Note the lady in hoop-skirt, and a few passengers who have still not boarded the train.

THE "ATLANTIC AND PACIFIC" AT CAPE HORN

The spectacular view of the American River Canyon from Cape Horn led to the custom, observed for many years, of stopping trains there so that the passengers could step out and look at the view. This picture is of the 1870's.

Thus pushed, the railhead spurted on. Up to Dutch Flat the average rate had been only a mile and a half per month. In the next fifteen miles this rate was more than doubled, and the railhead was established at Cisco on November 24, 1866. There it rested until the construction over the pass was completed.

By now, Crocker had more than ten thousand men at the work. Little one-horse dump carts were the chief means of moving dirt. But the methods were up-to-date by the standards of the time. Though drills were driven by hand, explosives were freely used. Crocker boasted, "We burned 500 kegs of powder in about half-a-mile distance every day, throwing off the rocks." When the granite, encountered from Cisco onward, proved too tough for ordinary powder, Crocker brought in a Scottish technician to manufacture nitroglycerin. The magnificent forest along the right of way was cut down ruthlessly to supply ties, timber for trestles, and fuel for the wood-burning locomotives.

VIEW OF CAPE HORN

Since a good photographic view of Cape Horn would require a day's walking by a photographer, the more fanciful artist (G. M. Ottinger, again) supplies the deficiency. His war-bonneted Indians in statuesque pose are thrown in for good measure.

VIEW FROM CAPE HORN—1868

This technical triumph by an early photographer, probably Alfred Hart, manages to show both the close-up engine and the distant landscape in focus. Note the Civil War cap.

STILL MORE OF CAPE HORN

More realistic than the preceding picture, this one is at least partly copied from photographs. The locomotives are accurately rendered. Some Chinese laborers with their wheelbarrows have been supplied for foreground.

By the next summer, sixteen miles were finished beyond Cisco, plus two miles on the east slope, constructed by workmen who had been taken over the pass and kept supplied by the wagon road.

Finally, in June 1868, the mountain section was completed. The pass that Elisha Stevens had discovered, only twenty-four years before, was conquered by a railroad. (Stevens himself, about sixty-five years old, was living a hermit-like existence on a small ranch near Bakersfield, interested in poultry and bees. He was unknown to fame, and no one invited him to attend the opening of the railroad across the pass.)

During the rest of 1868 and the early months of 1869, the builders raced ahead across the easy country of Nevada. Then came the joining with the Union Pacific and the driving of the Gold Spike on May 10, 1869. The route across Donner Pass was established as an essential link in world-transportation. Conductors on trains leaving Sacramento could now call out proudly to their passengers: "Take your seats for New York and intermediate stations!"

But the pass that had almost stopped Elisha Stevens and had wrecked the Donners still had a trick left. In his advocacy of the route, Judah had been over-optimistic in considering that the snow would not be much of a difficulty. Immediately,

LONG RAVINE TRESTLE

A mile north of Colfax the railroad crosses Long Ravine. (See picture on page 54.) In the 1870s the Nevada County Narrow Gauge Railroad ran beneath this trestle, and the photographer has here seized the chance to get a picture showing trains on both lines. The modern four-lane highway now crosses beneath the railroad at the same point, but the old wooden structure has been replaced by one of steel.

however, it became evident that the maintenance of traffic throughout the winter was a major problem. The simple push-plows, which were all that were then available, even when run at a drift with the whole force of several locomotives behind them, proved inadequate to keep the tracks clear. The answer was the building of many miles of snowsheds, constructed of timbers heavy enough to withstand the dead weight of many feet of snow. These sheds were not only expensive, but also obstructed the view of the passengers and frequently caught fire. Nevertheless, the problem of snow-removal has remained an acute one, for the highway as well as for the railroad. (See illustrations.)

Since the building of the railroad, the Donner Pass region has never lapsed into its primitive condition. The Donner Lake area soon became a summer resort. The opening of the railroad, however, killed off the Dutch Flat-Donner Lake road, which lapsed into disuse and became almost impassable. For about forty years the railway held undisputed sway. Only after the development of the automobile did there begin to be a renewed interest in a highway. In 1909, going over the old road, the state engineer reported it in such abominable condition that one could scarcely call it a road at all.

From that year on, the story has been one of continual change and improvement. The first work was merely to make the old road passable throughout. But even in the second two decades of the twentieth century, standards of what consti-tuted a sufficiently good mountain road were extremely low. In 1920, when the author first drove over the pass, the so-called Victory Highway rated as a main route, but was still primi-tive. It was, as far as he remembers, a two-way road on which cars could pass almost anywhere, but it was largely unpaved, and the drop-off at the pass was so spectacular as to be almost terrifying.

Major work commenced in 1923, when a new grade was constructed up the steep east face of the pass. In 1925, the old Dog Valley detour, established in 1845, was finally eliminated, and cars began to go through upper Truckee canyon, where

THE ROAD—1890-1960

The upper picture shows the Dutch Flat-Donner Lake Road after it had been superseded by the railroad and allowed to go to pieces. The surface has washed away, leaving the broad and solid foundation. This last is so well located and so firmly built that it has been utilized by the modern two-lane highway. Tree-growth has changed almost beyond recognition.

PLEASURE BOATS—1890

As soon as the railroad rendered it accessible, the Donner Lake area began to develop as a summer resort. Note derby hats, and small steam launch.

the Stevens party had passed. Through the twenties and into the thirties work continued.

To tell just when a "modern" highway was completed is difficult, because there has scarcely been a time when certain sections were not in need of improvement to be brought up to the general standards. By the middle thirties, however, the highway was a beautiful and pleasant road to drive, perhaps all the more interesting because a few twisty sections of the old wagon road were still in use, though now paved. Anyone who knew the country will look back to the years just before the Second World War as a golden age. The highway was plenty good enough for anyone not in a roaring hurry, and the traffic was seldom excessive. Moreover, the road was still adjusted to the country, not imposed upon it. This period also saw the rapid development of the region as a vacation area—for summer residents, and even more particularly for people coming for winter sports.

After 1945, with the rapid increase of population in California and with the even more rapid development of highway transportation, especially trucking, the highway which had seemed adequate became dangerously antiquated. The only solution was the construction of a modern four-lane freeway. In some places, the jump was made without an intermediate stage. Thus, above Auburn, a section which had not been much relocated since it was first laid out was suddenly reconstructed as a freeway. Whether the present freeway, not as yet completed (1960), will be the final word, or whether, indeed, it will even remain adequate for many years, must still remain doubtful.

GETTING A TREE OUT

In this picture of logging in Nevada County, probably about 1890, a ten-horse team is harnessed to a solid-wheeled wagon on which are three sections of a magnificent Ponderosa pine. Oxen were frequently used in the woods instead of horses.

The history of road transportation across the pass, thus shows four stages—the emigrant road, the Dutch Flat-Donner Lake road, the "old" two-lane highway, the four-lane freeway. The story of the railroad is simpler, since the original line has never been replaced, though it has been supplemented with a second track, sometimes built at a distance from the original one, so that there is a "down" line and an "up" line. One should also remember that a telegraph line was built along with the railroad. Later came the main transcontinental lead of the

TREES

Because of lumbering, few large trees remain along the highway. Here, near Yuba Gap, some big Jeffrey pines give some indication of what the forest originally was.

telephone line, which was a prominent feature along the highway before it was put underground to avoid being constantly damaged by the heavy winter snows. An electric power-line also makes use of the pass, and a pipeline has been constructed. One of the standard air routes also crosses at this point.

In general, therefore, the keynote for the whole area has been transportation. Out of the opportunity to cross the mountains at this point, the whole history of the region has developed. Thus, also, it remains. Even the heavy use of the region for skiing results not from its being better than other areas, but

HIGHWAY—1914

Even though some improvements had been made by 1914, the highway was still primitive. Note the advertisement painted on the rocks. The tree at the right is a western white pine; that in the distance, a juniper.

HIGHWAY—1932

This shows the same grade that is still being used (1960). There is as yet no paving.

OBSERVATION POINT AND BRIDGE

Approximately at the top of the pass, the observation point and bridge are famous spots on the transcontinental run of U. S. 40. Note that even in 1938 tourists had been doing their best to destroy the beauty of the place by dumping garbage over the wall.

from the easy accessibility offered by a major highway which is kept open throughout the winter.

Donner Pass has its beauty, of high crags and gleaming granite; the view eastward across the lake is justly famous. Every effort should be made to preserve these beauties, to give them continued protection from billboards, to prevent the blackening of the country by fires, and to cover up the unsightly scars often resulting from highway construction.

Yet even if it had remained wholly untouched by man, the country of the pass would not have equalled Yosemite and other areas for Alpine beauty. It has kept a rendezvous with history, and its interest to the person who passes here should be historical as much as scenic. At the summit, for instance, one can enjoy the beauty of the view, but can also see the remains of

FOUR-LANE HIGHWAY

In 1959 the four-lane highway was being constructed rapidly. It is here seen between Colfax and Gold Run. The over-crowded two-lane highway shows at the right.

two primitive roads in addition to the present highway, can look across at the railroad, and can also know that the emigrant wagons were dragged up somewhere to reach the same gap. The present volume has attempted to relate the story of how all this came to be.

Winter World

EW PLACES DISPLAY such a contrast between seasons as does Donner Pass. In summer, the tourist sees a sunny and beneficent landscape. In winter, one storm follows another until snow has piled up to almost incredible depths. No other region commonly frequented by man equals this one in the depths of its snow. In 1937-38 the fall at Norden totaled 805 inches, or more than 67 feet. Snow in the Sierra consolidates and settles between storms, but the depth on the ground at a particular time is often more than twenty feet.

The "bad" winters are remembered in the history and folktale of the pass. The first one to be recorded was that of 1846-47, the year of the Donner Party. Among its notable successors have been 1889-90, 1937-38, and 1951-52.

The following pictures give some idea both of the terror and of the beauty of a Sierran winter. One should remember, however, that effective photography is impossible during a storm, so that the pictures produce more of an impression of calm than is really warranted.

PUSH-PLOW

A simple push-plow is here seen in deep snow near Cisco in 1867.

AUGER-PLOW

This so-called cyclone snow plow was developed and tried during the heavy winter of 1889-90. It was not successful in boring its way through the drifts, and was soon abandoned in favor of the rotary plow.

EARLY METHODS ON THE RAILROAD

In the 1870's only push-plows were available, and the approved technique was to rush the snow and attempt to throw it from the track by main force. Here seven wood-burning locomotives work behind a plow on the track west of Truckee.

THE BIG WINTER—1889-90

During this winter the railroad was blocked for four months. The track was finally cleared in March by the newly invented rotary plows. These pictures, near Cisco, show the clean cut made by the rotary in deep and heavily consolidated snow.

MORE OF THE BIG WINTER

These pictures, taken at same time and place as those on the preceding page, show more rotary work and the shovelers swarming in for the clean-up.

SNOW SHED IN WINTER

In still another picture of the big winter the photographer is more interested in his interplay of light and shadow than in mere demonstration of depth of snow.

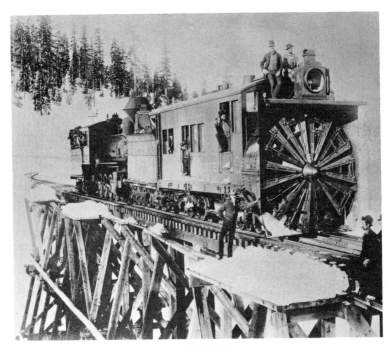

ROTARY PLOW

This type of plow was developed during the big winter of 1889-90, and has remained standard snow-removal equipment. Picture taken probably in 1890.

WRECKED SNOW SHED

In the winter of 1931-32 a slide developed enough weight and force to carry away a section of snow shed, leaving the wreckage of heavy beams scattered about on the mountainside.

NORDEN—WINTER, 1936

This is like one of those old-fashioned puzzles, "Find the dog!" One could almost say also, "Find the house!" The trees are mostly firs.

STALLED STREAMLINER

In January, 1952, the streamliner *City of San Francisco* was stalled (See next page).

STALLED STREAMLINER

On the morning of January 13, 1952, the *City of San Francisco* was stalled near the highway maintenance station at Yuba Gap. A blizzard was raging with winds up to 100 miles per hour. The plight of the 200 passengers and crew was not considered serious until afternoon when the only railroad rotary close at hand was overwhelmed by a snow slide and its engineer killed. Hope then rested in a single highway rotary, which had already been overworked and had suffered a breakdown. This rotary was some eight miles down the road, its crew already worn down by round-the-clock work. Because of the never-ceasing blizzard the rotary only fought its way through, heroically, to make contact at eight o'clock on January 16, when matters were becoming critical on the train. The stranded passengers and crewmen were thus narrowly prevented from becoming another Donner Party.

SNOW CLEARANCE—ROTARY

A rotary is at work in March, 1936, near Donner Summit. Note wind-swept trees (Jeffrey pines) just managing to maintain themselves under Arctic conditions close to timberline around 7000 feet. The wisps of cirrus cloud give indication of an approaching storm, and blowing snow shows that the wind is already high.

WINTER VIEW
FROM
THE SUMMIT

Two rotaries are
at work, and the
road has just been
rendered passable
in a moderate
depth of snow.

NIGHT CLEARANCE

The walls of snow are here more than twelve feet high.

AFTER THE STORM

In the still cold that follows a storm, beneath a clear blue sky, two rotaries are at work widening the cut in preparation for the next storm. This is at about the 6000-foot level, among the firs.

BURIED CARS

Parked cars, later covered with snow, are often a hazard to the work of rotaries, and are always an embarrassment to the owners, who have no recourse but to dig them out with shovels.

SKIERS' PARKING

Such over-crowded conditions as this on the highway near Soda Springs suggest the disaster that might occur if a sudden storm should maroon so many people. The forest is of firs with a few big Jeffrey pines interspersed.

OPEN TO TRAFFIC

In this picture, taken in March, 1951, at about 6000 feet, the snow-plows are still at work, but heavy traffic is moving through. The forest here is of mixed pines and firs.

ROAD CLOSED!

Trucks and cars are here lined up at Baxter waiting for the road to be
opened over the pass.

WINTER OF '51-'52

This dramatic picture, taken on January 17, 1952, during a lull, shows
two rotaries working slowly toward each other to open a section of
the highway a mile west of Emigrant Gap. Even here on the flat-
topped ridge the snow is about twenty feet deep. The dull sky indicates
that the weather has not cleared. The highway had already been closed
since January 11. Other storms followed, and the road across the pass
was blocked for a total period of six weeks, the longest interruption of
traffic since modern snow-clearance began.

NARROW LANE

On January 26, 1952, four days after the preceding picture, only a narrow lane had been opened, and the road was still closed to traffic.

SNOW WALLS

In March, 1952, the road was technically open, but conditions were still polar, as here seen on the grade up to the summit.

WINTER WONDERLAND

This is another picture taken on January 26, 1952, during the lull between storms, when there was hope that the highway could be soon opened. During such lulls the air is clear and the scenes are often of extraordinary beauty. Note here the snow-stakes which mark the line of the road.

CAVE-IN

Still another picture of January 26, 1952. The rotary is here methodically getting rid of snow that has tumbled down from the high wall on the side.

TRUCK IN TROUBLE

This picture displays conditions sometime during 1952 on the grade up the east face of the pass.

MACHINE AGAINST WINTER

Here, in February, 1952, a single rotary labors against what seems a whole continent of snow. The scene is just below the top of the pass. Note wrecked trailer at right.

JANUARY 22, 1952

This picture shows a snow-depth of about 20 feet at the summit. At this time the road had been closed for nine days and because of continuing storms was not reopened for five weeks more.

"PARK OFF PAVEMENT"

Although one should not argue with a policeman, this particular injunction was difficult when the wall of snow along the highway was about 15 feet high, on March 23, 1952.

SPRINGTIME ON THE PASS

In May, 1941, snow had melted somewhat, and there was no problem of maintenance, except for the possibility of a late storm.

SQUAW VALLEY

An early historian wrote: "Squaw Valley is the most beautiful valley the eye of man ever beheld." It was at one time called Ladies Paradise. Its beauty is still apparent, and it has become even more famous as the seat of the 1960 Winter Olympics. The 1959 Trial Events are here pictured, together with a general view.

"WITH THE GREATEST OF EASE"

Since the 1930's skiing has been a major sport in the Donner Pass area. This picture is from the Trial Events (1959) for the 1960 Winter Olympic Games to be held at Squaw Valley.

Another scene from the Trial Events for the 1960 Winter Olympic games.

Competitor in men's downhill course in Olympic Trial Events at Squaw Valley, 1959. Note snow clinging to the fir trees to make the characteristic "snow ghosts" of the Sierra winter.

Place Names

MANY PLACES in the area are descriptively named from appearance or some other characteristic, or from real or fancied resemblance to another place. Here we have Red Mountain, Castle Peak, Summit Valley, Liberty Cap (so appearing when seen from the southwest), Crystal Lake, Big Bend (of the Yuba River), Dutch Flat (because a German lived on a rather level spot), Cape Horn (a difficult promontory for the railroad to get around), Gold Run, Soda Springs (the springs are some miles to the south), Sugar Bowl, Blue Canyon, Andesite Ridge (for the kind of rock found there). Tahoe is a Washo Indian word, meaning "lake." Sierra Nevada is Spanish, meaning "range snowed-on," or merely "snowy range." Nevada City and County in California were named from the mountains in 1850 and 1851; the name was applied to the region farther east when Nevada Territory was organized in 1861.

Some places take names from an incident which happened there. Emigrant Gap records the fact that there the emigrants lowered their wagons to Bear Valley through a gap in a ridge. The American River was named by the famous Captain Sutter because some American trappers used to cross at a ford there. Bear River and Rattlesnake Creek probably indicate, not any special abundance of those animals, but merely someone's encounter with a bear or a rattlesnake. Squaw Valley may be similarly named, or because some particular Indian woman, now unknown to history, once lived there. Boreal Ridge is probably no colder than any other ridge; most likely the man who named it suffered from a cold north wind when he was there.

Many names are those of people who were associated with the area. We have already met Donner, Colfax, Schallenberger, Judah and Truckee. J. J. Cisco was treasurer of the Central Pacific. Norden, Lake Van Norden, and Lake Spaulding were named for water-company officials, Charles Van Norden and John Spaulding. Reno was named for General J. L. Reno of the Union army, who was killed at South Mountain in 1862. Weimar (still locally pronounced weé-mer) was called for an Indian chief whose name was originally written as Weimah; it was later spelled as if derived from the German city.

The Yuba River bears the name of an Indian tribe which once lived on its banks in the Sacramento Valley. The stream followed by the highway is really the South Fork, Sierran rivers being notable for their remarkable development of "fork" names.

Auburn was named nostagically for their home town by miners who had come from Auburn, New York. Illinoistown and Hampshire Rocks also seem to be retrospectively named.

Many of the old mining camps bore bizarre names. In many cases these must have been bestowed because of some incident, of which the record has not been preserved. You Bet and Red Dog are examples; the latter probably commemorates a favorite card game among the Forty-niners, not a canine. Secrettown, Secret Ravine, etc., were probably so called because some miner made a strike and tried to keep it secret.

Baxter is a good example of a name which has merely evolved. Now a well-recognized place name because of the location there of the gates by which the highway is blocked when snowed in, it was originally nothing but the name of the restaurant and overnight stopping-place located there.

Shaping
of the Landscape

HE ALERT VISITOR to the Donner Pass area is always impressed by the cliff-like rise on the eastern face of the pass, as contrasted with the gradual slope on the west. This results from the manner of formation of the range, which consists of a block of the earth's surface some hundreds of miles long and about eighty miles wide, which has been raised along its eastern side—much as if one had tipped a short plank along one edge.

After this elevation, the glacial epochs occurred, and in four succeeding periods Donner Pass was covered with a large ice-field. The last one is estimated to have been 250 square miles in area. Long glaciers extended down the valley where Donner Lake now lies and also in the other direction along the line of the highway. Some of the higher peaks stuck up through the ice, and thus still display the rough and craggy appearance of rock which has not been planed off by ice. Around Big Bend the smooth rounded elevations, on the contrary, show the features resulting from ice-work. The glacier which descended to the east rested for a long time with its end in the same place, and deposited its debris there in a terminal moraine, thus forming the low natural dam behind which Donner Lake is impounded. Many small lakes, few of them visible from the highway, are characteristic of the glaciated country. Erratic rocks, deposited by the melting ice, may be seen in the vicinity of Big Bend.

Since the ice-sheets swept the country bare at no very great period in the past (perhaps 25,000 years), soil has had little chance to accumulate, and the beautiful shining granite surfaces are a feature of the region. Tree-growth is correspondingly scanty. Looking eastward from Emigrant Gap, one can get a fairly clear view of the largely bare glaciated granite country and the heavily-forested unglaciated country.

Since glaciers carve broad-bottomed valleys, the highway is able to follow close to the Yuba River without difficulty for some miles west of the summit. Then, west of Big Bend, the road enters a narrow stream-cut canyon, and has been constructed along its edge, with difficulty, by being blasted out of the rock.

There are less obvious evidences of glaciation as far as Emigrant Gap, but west of that point the highway passes through a different kind of country. Here the streams have cut deep canyons. The great gorge of the North Fork of the American River (to the south) is in places 3,000 feet deep, steep-sided, and V-shaped. Since the road follows the generally broad and comparatively flat-topped ridge, the motorist is seldom conscious of these deep canyons, though he may have fleeting glimpses near Emigrant Gap and Colfax.

The famous view from Cape Horn results from the fact that at that point the railroad was forced to keep to the very edge of the ridge and even to cut out a passage a little way down the canyon-side. In this unglaciated region the soil on the ridge-tops is deep enough for an abundant tree-growth.

Animals and Plants

MANY DEER are present, but generally keep away from the heavily-traveled highway. This is fortunate, since a high-speed collision with a deer is a serious matter. An occasional black or brown bear may still be found, but the famous California grizzly is extinct. The larger predators include mountain lions and coyotes. Much small game exists, but seldom makes an appearance. The principal fish is the beautiful and game rainbow trout.

Wild flowers are often abundant, particularly in the spring. At this time the delicate white sprays of ceanothus (wild lilac, or deer-brush) may cover whole hillsides.

Most notable to anyone passing along the highway is the growth of coniferous trees. The different species keep to fairly well-marked zones, according to altitude. Mingling with the oaks, and first to appear (at under 1,000 feet on the western slope), are the so-called Digger pines—scraggly-looking, bearing large cones and long, gray-green needles, never attaining much size or majesty. From 2,000 to 4,000 feet the Ponderosa, or Western Yellow Pine, is the commonest species. When mature, six to eight feet in diameter, conspicuously displaying its yellow bark, this is a magnificent tree. Along the highway there has been so much lumbering that these pines seldom are more than a foot or two in diameter; even so, many of them are handsome trees. Mingled with them are Douglas firs and incense cedars. The sugar pine, largest of pines and very valuable for timber, has been largely logged off. An occasional one may be seen, with its long cones, popular for souvenirs, dangling from the ends of the branches.

Around 4,000 feet the white firs begin to predominate. Beautifully trim and neat when young (and therefore popular for Christmas trees) these seldom attain large size, and grow less attractive with age. Still higher, red firs, difficult to distinguish from the whites when young, also appear.

At higher altitudes the Jeffrey pine, a more hardy species, supplants the Ponderosa, which it so much resembles as often to be indistinguishable except to the trained eye. In general, the largest specimens to be seen along the highway at present are Jeffrey pines. They are magnificent trees, though their slightly reddish bark is not so striking as the yellow bark of the mature Ponderosas.

Above 5,000 feet the climate grows increasingly rigorous, and the bare rock surfaces provide little soil. Tree-growth occurs only in favorable locations, particularly in stream-bottoms. The Jeffrey pine still grows magnificently, but the commonest tree is the lodgepole pine, which favors slightly moist places and grows in thick stands. It is recognizable by its "tightly stretched" bark, but it seldom grows into a very striking tree.

At the very top of the pass a few Alpine species appear, usually as rather stunted individuals. Here occur the Western white pine and the juniper. The latter even roots courageously in a mere rock crevice, and may grow for a century without attaining more than a few feet in height.

SOURCES OF PICTURES

By courtesy of California Division of Highways, pictures on pages 59, 60, 61, 70 (upper), 72, 73, 74, 75, 76, 77, 78, 79, 80, 81, 82, 83, 84; by courtesy of Southern Pacific Company, pictures on pages 28, 38, 42, 43, 44, 46, 47, 48, 49 (upper), 50, 51, 52 (lower), 54, 64, 65, 66, 67, 68, 69; picture on page 32, by courtesy of Sutter's Fort Museum; by courtesy of California State Library, pictures on pages 34, 35, 36, 37, 40, 58; by courtesy of Organizing Committee, VIII Olympic Winter Games, pictures on pages 85, 86, 87, 88; by courtesy of Bancroft Library, pictures on pages 10, 18, 22, 24, 26, 27, 28, 29, 30, 31, 33, 41, 49 (lower), 56 (upper), 57; pictures on pages 1, 2, 12, 13, 15, 16, 17, 19, 20, 33, 39, 45, 56, 62, 96 are by the author; picture on page 56 (upper) is by Victor L. Dorsey; pictures on pages 29 and 30 are by Susy Lewis; picture of Schallenberger on page 8 is from San Jose *Pioneer*, Apr. 15, 1893; picture of Stevens on page 8 is from San Francisco *Daily Evening Post*, Dec. 23, 1883; the sketches on pages 49 and 52 are by G. M. Ottinger in *Nelson's Pictorial Guide Book;* picture on page 53 is from *Frank Leslie's Illustrated Newspaper*, Apr. 27, 1878; pictures on pages 26 and 27 are from Thompson and West's *History of Nevada County*. The pictures on pages 12, 13, 20 and 96 are used by courtesy of the University of California Press; that on page 4 by courtesy of the Houghton Mifflin Company.

The early pictures furnished by the Southern Pacific Company are, probably all of them, the work of Alfred Hart, official photographer for the railroad during its construction and immediately afterwards.

EMIGRANT CROSSING

Rust marks left by wheels on the rough granite slope indicate that the emigrants here hauled their wagons up. The "true pass" is just to the right, off the picture. The high point is Donner Peak (8019 feet).